BREATHE MY HEART

Quote And Prose

L.C. Raker

ISBN-13: 9798353536284
ISBN-10: 1477123456

Cover design by: Art Painter
Library of Congress Control Number: 2018675309
Printed in the United States of America

To all the ones, who have love with all their heart

"Wiith every beat of my heart, new sayings part."
-LC Raker

CONTENTS

Title Page

Copyright

Dedication

Epigraph

I.   1

II.   2

III.   3

IV.   4

V.   5

VI.   6

VII.   7

VIII.   8

IX.   9

X.   10

XI.   11

XII.   12

XIII.   13

XIV. 14

XV. 15

XVI. 16

XVII. 17

XVIII. 18

XIX. 19

XX. 20

XXI. 21

XXII. 22

XXIII. 23

XXIV. 24

XXV. 25

XXVI. 26

XXVII. 27

XXVIII. 28

XXIX. 29

XXX. 30

XXXI. 31

XXXII. 32

XXXIII. 33

XXXIV. 34

XXXV. 35

XXXVI. 36

XXXVII. 37

XXVIII.	38
XXXIX.	39
XL.	40
XLI.	41
XLII.	42
XLIII.	43
XLIV.	44
XLV.	45
XLVI.	46
XLVII.	47
XLVIII.	48
XLIX.	49
L.	50
LI.	51
LII.	52
LIII.	53
LIV.	54
LV.	55
LVI.	56
LVII.	57
LVIII.	58
LIX.	59
LX.	60
LXI.	61

LXII.   62

LXIII.   63

LXIV.   64

LXV.   65

LXVI.   66

LXVII.   67

LXVIII.   68

LXIX.   69

LXX.   70

LXXI.   71

LXXII.   72

LXXIII.   73

LXXIV.   74

LXV.   75

LXXVI.   76

LXXVII.   77

LXXXVIII.   78

LXXXIX.   79

XC.   80

XCI.   81

XCII.   82

XCIII.   83

XCIV.   84

XCV.   85

XCVI.	86
XCVII.	87
XCVIII.	88
XCIX.	89
C.	90
CI.	91
CII.	92
CIII.	93
CIV.	94
CV.	95
CVI.	96
CVII.	97
CVIII.	98
CIX.	99
CXI.	100
CXII.	101
Books By This Author	103
About The Author	105

I.

Just walk away

Know it's days past

Never could you stay

It wouldn't of last

Know you lie

No longer do I cry

II.

III.

Been a mess

In my head

Need some rest

Thoughts of you

*

*

*

*

Instead

IV.

They said "Forget It"
But I can't not one bit

To keep my sanity in place
During an anxiety race
Reminisce of the night

Within my mind
Within seconds calmness
................I find

V.

I've tried to fight

This burning flame

Let us make this right

Forget who's to blame

VI.

Forever....
You will be...
The only one...
For me...

VII.

What could have been?

If we allowed our hearts to pretend...

The world couldn't take us in....

How our love would of never end...

VIII.

Let's make believe

Just for a moment for me

Where it was only us....

Lost once again in each other's eyes

Way before our endless cries

Where we could be....

Together again

Before this sad end

IX.

Don't want to be...

Just a memory
Or a passing...
Story

I want an...
End

To enable me...
To mend

X.

Guess to keep your promises....

It's on my dime...

Unlike some people...

I don't waste my money or my time...

XI.

As once a beauty you were to me....

Inside as ugly as ugly can be....

XII.

Sad to think...

You feel...

I'm messing with your heart

When I've always felt this way ....

From the start

The words I spoke were ....

Genuine and true

But most of all, I loved you

XIII.

Never had a chance

Should of left, before it started

I made a daring stance

But you just parted.

XIV.

Show my heart....

Never got a chance...

Before you had to part.

XV.

Don't

Know

What

Say?

To

Have

You

Stay.

XVI.

I love my heart

How tragical they say

How it ended, before it starts

Magical I say

But couldn't stay

XVII.

Why do I ...
Smile

Cause nothing will ....
Change

I still will...
Love, Care, and understand

With or without you...
Distance, time away means nothing

If the love is true...
That I thought you knew

XVIII.

Wish I can take you back...

To where it all begins...

And fully let you in...

XIX.

A moment for me...

Meant a love to be...

Don't you see...

XX.

It's not the distance...

But the fact...

You never acknowledge...

My existence

XXI.

The knot within

Which seems to turn...

Is your sin

I wish to burn...

XXII.

Wouldn't of vow a love so true...

If back, then...
I knew the real you...

XXIII.

Behold my heart...

No longer.....

....pitter.... patters

Since you tore it apart

XXIV.

The Melody of my soul is...
In the chords of your heart

XXV.

My love was real...

Unfortunately...

The cards were a bad deal

XXVI.

It is not by sight...

But by the soul...

We see love's light...

XXVII.

What your eyes behold...

        May not shimmer, or be gold

Though the beats of my heart...

        Plays in the presence of your sight

Lights the evening air...

        So Bright

XXVIII.

All which remains....

> *Is*
>
> *A*
>
> *Heart*
>
> *In*
>
> *Pain*

XXIX.

A heal heart

And a strong soul

Will fight any storm...

As you age old

XXX.

For What I scribble...

Could be an emotion past

One sending a trigger ripple

Pen to paper for it don't last

XXXI.

How about being in my place?

Where you were the last to know...

The one who made your heartache...

Made you a fool and ran a show...

XXXII.

Beauty once saw...

Within your eyes

No Longer sparkle...

Like the night sky

XXXIII.

If my arms....

Could heal your soul

I'd never...

Let you go

XXXIV.

Never Stay

If it changes you

Start a new

Let's start today

XXXV.

Embrace your heart

It links to your soul

XXXVI.

Love The one...

Who wouldn't hurt you

XXXVII.

I'll

Always love you...

There nothing I can do...

XXVIII.

People say "When you love someone, it's about actions"

Though, the silences of my heart

Contradicts that direction

XXXIX.

I know...

What is true...

But...

I just wanted to hear it from you

XL.

The song which plays

In the hearts of all

Haunts my days

Was my downfall

XLI.

No point …

To ask…

If there's…

No Response

XLII.

A Love of a lifetime...

Will bring calmness

To your mind

XLIII.

I must really give out...
A lonely vibe
The funny part is...
I'm truly fine
Just prefer ...
Not to mingle
And
Have my energy be...
Drain by nonsense

XLIV.

Made the choice

You felt was right

Use to have an angelic voice

Made a mistake that night

But your wrong

Only made me strong

XLV.

How people praise you?

This is so true...

But no one knows...

The real you...

XLVI.

This is me…

An attention grab …
Is so naïve

I rather sit…

In a

Corner
And
Observe

XLVII.

I've

Always

Love

You

But you never saw me...

XLVIII.

XLVII.

I'd rather you break my heart

Leave and part....

I'll be able to handle it...

Unlike some,

Who would just fall apart.

XLIX.

The beautiful words…

You spoke

Now makes me choke.

L.

Quite a dream…

You were to me…

Almost believe…

We would be…

LI.

Our love was like...

A flower

Blossom in...

The Summer Breeze...

Wilted in ...

The Winter Freeze

LII.

Your brown eyes…

Turned blue…

And in return

I played

Your fool…

LIII.

I was silent

You loved someone else

It didn't stop...

The beats ...

Of my heart...

Even though...

It was torn apart.

LIV.

Love my heart...
Love my mind...
Never will I part...

LV.

Spoken words...

From my heart...

So true this day...

As it was from the start

LVI.

Has been yours

From the start

Still beats your memory

Since you part

LVII.

Not Jealous, mad

To you, my emotions don't matter

Who cares if I'm sad

And my heart was shattered

LVIII.

A one-night stand…

That held your hand…

Smile at you

Care so true

In the end…

You couldn't even be my friend

LIX.

The

Kiss

Made

Light

Blinded

Love

First

Sight

LX.

Love is not a fairytale

I don't play make believe

LXI.

For if the love is true...

The person will always love you.

LXII.

Love

Is

Easy

Hard

Love

Isn't

From

Heaven

Above

LXIII.

May I pen like a fool...

But I know real love...

Isn't cruel

LXIV.

It's trauma

Your memory

Because there no end to the story..

LXV.

People say
"Love is a foolish dream"
Then you haven't met....
The one it seems

LXVI.

In love...

Give your all...

But that should have been there...

When you fall...

I question...

Was it love at all?

LXVII.

Every time, my eyes identify you

My heart begins to beat.

LXVIII.

Want to take …

One last spin

All you have to say is …

"Let me in."

LXIX.

Find the truth...
Within the lies.

Find the love...
Within the hurt.

Find your way...
Through
The storm

Created from...
The night.

LXX.

What lies within your eyes

All the answers ...

To my questions why's...

LXXI.

Finding out what is true...

Starts with just....

one question from you

LXXII.

I know

What is true...

But do

You...

LXXIII.

The

Beating

Of

My

Heart

Doesn't

Stop

Cause

You

Had

To

Part.

LXXIV.

Unlike

You

I'm

Too

Old…

for your games.

LXV.

Oh! You miss me...

What a shame...

Should have thought

About it

Before you ran

Your game

LXXVI.

I miss you

I love you

I care about you

But not afraid of losing you...

LXXVII.

Words are penned…

To always remember you…

My Friend.

LXXXVIII.

The difference…

Between you and me…

I can face the truth…

How about you?

LXXXIX.

Words spoken so true...

I don't expect from you

XC.

XC.

Countless tries...

No answers why...

XCI.

Decades old...

Still, you plague my soul...

Is it from your lies?

How you never tried?

Does it matter to me?

More than it did to thee.

XCII.

Love cannot be defined

It's a perspective etch in our minds.

XCIII.

Distance

Is

An

Excuse

For

The

Weak

Hearted.

XCIV.

If I could heal your soul...

By just the touch of my hand.

XCV.

In the beginning of the night...

Before the stars appear...

My heart

Beats...

XCVI.

A Melody for you...

My dear...

XCVII.

Had my heart...

From the start...

Till this day...

You're still my favorite piece of art.

XCVIII.

I said, "It will always be."

I still love you...

Don't you see...

XCIX.

What is true?

My

Heart

Still

Resides

With

You...

C.

Maybe realize I tried...

As you just sat there and cried...

CI.

Waited years...

Expect more my dear...

But we did fear...

Feelings we held near...

CII.

When I look back...

Know nothing stays the same

But I want you to know

Neither of us,

are to blame

CIII.

Wish I could make this all go away...
All I can say is
"I'm Sorry"
 I left that day.

CIV.

Everyone:

If I knew then, what I know now

Me:

There wouldn't have been a final bow.

CV.

It is not about another chance....

Together, we had our final dance....

Gave my all, many times....

But I wasn't worth the climb

CVI.

No longer, do I cry
No longer, do I try

Even if I gave my all…
Your actions still stall
Don't have time for your games at all.

CVII.

Why am I mad at you?
Not the both of you.
One didn't play with my heart
And then decide to part.

CVIII.

No one knows...

Still allow people to think...

How amazing you are...

Why because you're a star...

Even though...

My heart you shatter...

To people you are their lifeline...

That is all that matters...

CIX.

As mad as I can be...

I still love and care about thee...

I hate that about me...

CXI.

Next Time, you run a game

Remember...

Someone's heart will never be the same.

CXII.

Just look in my eyes...

See the truth...

Not her lies...

BOOKS BY THIS AUTHOR

The Lingering Y's: Poetry From One Night Forlorn

The Snow Don't Last Forever

Mystical Lights

Some Roses Have Thorns

ABOUT THE AUTHOR

L. C. Raker

L.C. Raker is a residence of Northwest Indiana, originally from the south suburbs of Chicago. As far as she can recall, she has enjoy picking up a pen and scribbling her latest thoughts. She  enjoys nature and loves to read a good novel in her spare time.

This is her fifth book and her first book which will be available in all formats. This is also her first time writing saying and prose instead of full length. Little saying in a rhyming format, which will touch the heart and mind.

She been keeping busy this year in additional to her poetry, she is working on two full length novels, which is plan to be release in next year. She has two taboo novels which are available through Kindle Vella for the time being.